DOCTOR ON THE LINE

ISBN 1 871608 24 4

Published by

Irwell Press

3 Durley Avenue, Pinner, Middlesex, HA5 1JQ.

Printed by Amadeus Press, Huddersfield

DOCTOR
ON THE LINE

An East Anglian Railway Album

Dr. Ian C. Allen

IRWELL
PRESS

A Sunday Framlingham – Liverpool Street excursion at Framlingham, behind J15 0-6-0 No.65447 in the charge of driver Reg Crisp. With post-war petrol rationing these excursions were very popular. The train always stopped at Hacheston Halt, a typical ground level station composed of two sleepers and some cinders. The normal branch set was fitted with air-controlled steps to enable passengers to join and leave the train but the main line stock was not and, on Sundays, it was the Station Master's duty to see that his household steps were always put in the brake van of such excursions. It was then left to the guard to help any passengers joining or leaving the train up and down the steps. To ensure that I got a photo of this rather unusual procedure, I once persuaded a patient to take the excursion train. When she returned, she had greatly enjoyed the trip.

Dr. Ian C. Allen 1910 – 1989

Foreword

I should like to thank Mr. Richard Hardy for having made possible the stories behind so many of the photographs in this book . I first met him one wet November morning at Framlingham, thirty nine years ago, when he had been called away from moving into his new home at Ipswich, to re-rail the Framlingham branch locomotive. To move into a new home is one of life's most difficult tasks. To move in when it is raining is one of life's most unpleasant tasks. To be called away with the job uncompleted is almost to plumb the ultimate abyss. And yet there was Richard positively enjoying dealing with the problems connected with the re-railing.

Richard will always be remembered for being the first person to reveal to a fascinated world the joys and skills of firing. If he had been born a few years later, he would only have known diesel locomotives but, although he left it rather late, he had enough time to learn the art and to pass it on for posterity.

I should also like to thank Richard for having checked the technical facts in this book, and Mr. D. Mercer for having produced such excellent plates from my negatives – some of which are fifty to sixty years old.

Doctor Allen's manuscript was put into good order and many of the photographs made available through the efforts of his daughter, Mrs. Penelope Wickes. Mr. C. Moss of Ipswich saw to the collation of the various photographs and sought out remaining details from Dr. Allen's material, to enable a number of outstanding points to be resolved.

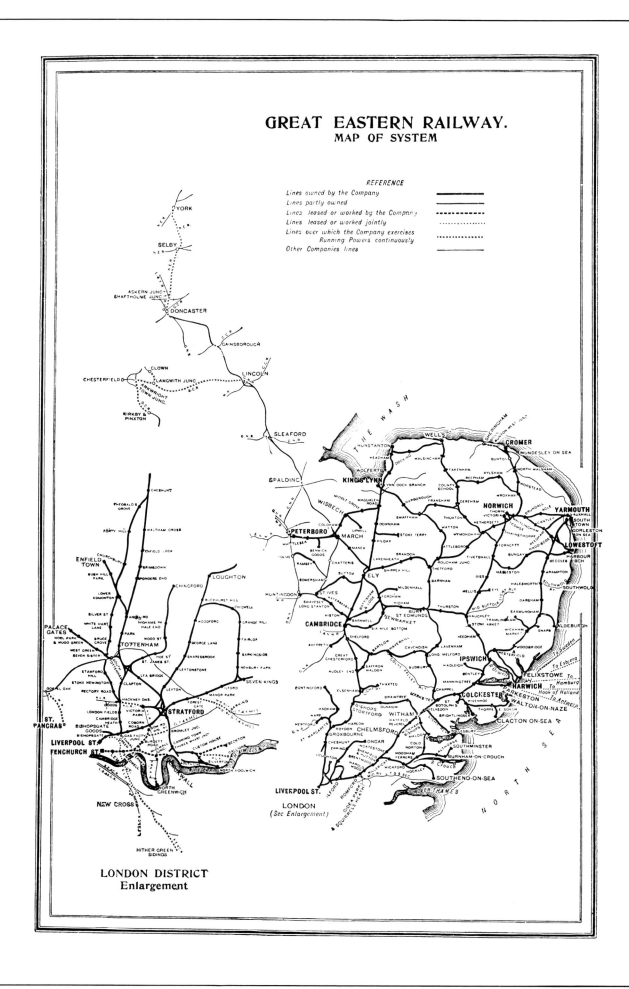

GREAT EASTERN RAILWAY.
MAP OF SYSTEM

REFERENCE

Lines owned by the Company
Lines partly owned
Lines leased or worked by the Company
Lines leased or worked jointly
Lines over which the Company exercises
  Running Powers continuously
Other Companies lines

LONDON DISTRICT
Enlargement

Liverpool Street is the London Terminus for East Anglia. The first plate shows the 15.36 to Clacton about to leave, hauled by Britannia 4-6-2 No. 70007 *Coeur de Lion*. To see it out, on the extreme right is Mr. Richard Hardy, at the time District Motive Power Superintendent. Then comes Passed Fireman Ron Eagle of Clacton, Inspector Ernie Foskett, Driver Bert Hudson of Clacton (who was travelling passenger) and Fireman Ron Cudmore of Clacton (next to locomotive). I had come up from Colchester early that morning and on showing my pass had been invited on to the footplate, but with a certain coolness. Just before we started the driver said 'where's your notebook?' Surprised, I said I had no notebook. I wanted to savour to the full every second of a lifelong ambition. He smiled warmly and said the last guest had filled three notebooks and had even told him how to drive his engine.

I have never read a good description of a footplate journey. Peter Handford has left his wonderful tape recordings of what it was like, but no one has ever adequately described the pulsating power which a driver has at his complete command. Thirty years ago there was scarcely a boy who, at some time of his life, had not wished to be an engine driver. Was this because on his engine, if nowhere else, he was master of his destiny, with only signalmen to thwart him? So, punctually, with Inspector Foskett as my guide, we started out of the station to be confronted immediately with Bethnal Green bank, and then right away for Norwich.

The Great Eastern Railway had always worked the world's greatest suburban service by steam, to which its successor, the LNER, had introduced in 1925 class N7 0-6-2 tanks. These were derived from a type introduced by the GER in 1915. This photo shows No.69605, built at Stratford in 1921, about to leave Liverpool Street for Chingford. There was always a hustle and bustle on the suburban side at Liverpool Street – different from the more peaceful main line platforms. Once safely up Bethnal Green bank the train would get under way with only a 45 mph slowing through Stratford station to impede it. Ahead lay Brentwood bank which, in by-gone days, would use up every ounce of steam the older locomotives were making. Foxes could often be seen crossing the line there.

Another view of Liverpool Street, which Mr. Malcolm Root has taken as the inspiration for his vivid painting – so vivid that you can almost smell the smokey atmosphere. Britannia No.70006 *Robert Burns* is getting ready to work the down Continental to Parkeston Quay, and Stratford's Sandringham 4-6-0 No.61611 *Raynham Hall* waits in the siding. The specially painted station pilot, N7 0-6-2T No.69614, can be seen under the soaring roof, which used to give such an inspiring start to so many travellers. Now, like Euston and Victoria, the trains seem to leave from dark and dismal dungeons.

Stratford, the locomotive works of the old GER, and its associated depot of several hundred locomotives, lay on the left hand side of the track of a down express. Railway lines seemed to run everywhere. It was reputed to be the most fascinating depot in the country, but only distant glimpses could be obtained of it from the train. A long, narrow, gas-lit tunnel ran from the station to the works and the shed, which had never made allowance for the increase in height of the average Eastender during the last century. In the nineteen-twenties and thirties the cab roofs of all the older GER locomotives had had to be raised to suit the greater height of the drivers. The first thing one saw on emerging from the tunnel was the breakdown train; the pilot engine, 0-6-2T No. 69653 stands ready to do a shunt with the 36ft crane and its riding van.

Then you would turn a corner and suddenly see a row of locomotives standing outside the Jubilee shed, all with steam ready for the evening rush hour: Britannia 4-6-2s Nos.70008 *Black Prince,* 70000 *Britannia* herself, B1s Nos.61384 (the Parkeston 'spare'), 61375, 61311 and a Class J19 0-6-0 waiting their call to duty. I once visited Stratford on a foggy November afternoon and came away amazed that any sort of train service could be run at all – the skill shown by all departments was unbelievable.

My favourite spot at Stratford was on the top of the coal chute. Class J69 0-6-0T No.68626 is standing as coal stage pilot; hundreds of tons of coal were required daily to feed the tenders of all the engines. One could climb up to the top of the chute to be rewarded by what must have been one of the best views in London. Here one could sit for hours watching the toy-like locomotives pottering about below.

Inspector Dick Elmer in the midst of the wild flowers that grew so surprisingly at Stratford. He is standing by Departmental 0-4-0T No. 33 which, at the time of the photo, was on loan for general use. These were powerful machines, but could never be driven fast. If they were, they would oscillate up and down and damage the cylinders on the rails. After one spell at the top of the tower Richard Hardy met me and introduced me to the driver of the EE Type 3 (Class 37) diesel that was going to take me down to Ipswich declaring "his mate makes the best cup of tea in East Anglia". He certainly did. It was on this occasion that just after Stratford, near Manor Park, a fox was lying in the sun on the railway bank with three cubs. Later one crossed the track in front of us on Brentwood bank.

The second photo from the Stratford coaling plant (it had been one of the first in the country) shows in the mid-ground engines of classes B12/3, K1, K3, 9F, B1, WD 2-8-0, J17, J19 and J39, quite a variety! In the background are long lines of GER-built steel 20 ton loco coal wagons used for internal coal working. The GER was a pioneer in the supply of these for loco coal; also in the background, amidst the pall of smoke are lines of GER 54ft suburban coaches, displaced by the Shenfield electrification. Most were converted in the mid-1950s into parcel vans and covered carriage trucks.

Class F6 2-4-2T No.67225 entering Braintree. It has at one time been fitted with a staff catching apparatus for working over the Midland and Great Northern Railway.

A J68 0-6-0T, No.68658. Built in 1923 with side windows in the cab, it was one of three sent to shunt in Boston Docks and was never fitted with either vacuum or Westinghouse brakes – nor with condensing apparatus. Two remained at Boston until replaced by diesel shunters. 68658 is shown working in the Stratford complex in 1958.

A down suburban train near Manor Park in 1936, hauled by F5 2-4-2T No.7180. It shows the original low cab roof, stove pipe chimney and double Ramsbottom safety valves. Brentwood bank was always a severe tax on a steam locomotive but, once over the top, it was a fast run down to Chelmsford and Witham, the junction for Braintree and Maldon.

Class J68 0-6-0 Tank No. 68666 working a Braintree to Witham train near Cressing. It was one of a batch built in 1923 for freight working, without condensing apparatus, and which had subsequently been fitted with the vacuum brake. Normally the Braintree yard shunter, 68666 was deputising for a failed F6 2-4-2T and itself developed a hot axle box shortly after the photo was taken, necessitating another loco being sent out urgently from Stratford. An F6 2-4-2 tank, of Route Availability 5, could work from Witham to Braintree but not to Maldon. On account of the trestle bridges on that line, its passage was restricted to Route Availability 4 locomotives such as the Class F5 2-4-2 tanks. A through train used to run from Liverpool Street to Maldon on Saturday afternoons, hauled by a Class J15 0-6-0. When the Britannias were introduced in 1951 an E4 2-4-0 was tried but in spite of their small wheels the J15s seem to have been more successful.

Beyond Witham, Kelvedon was the junction for the Tollesbury Light Railway. This is the branch train near Tollesbury hauled by J67 0-6-0T No.68608, one of three of the class which were never fitted with enlarged tanks. The branch coaches were saloon type and most uncomfortable. The first six-wheeled coach had originally come from the Stoke Ferry branch – the bogie coach had first been built in 1884 for the Wisbech and Upwell Tramway. The four-wheeled van at the end of the train sets the scale of the coaches. It is a Gresley pigeon van, built in 1928 at Stratford for use on the Great Eastern section. It is hard to realise that, in 1923, there were over ninety of these small 0-6-0 tank locomotives, some originally built in 1890, employed daily on the suburban passenger workings in and out of Liverpool Street. They were superseded in 1925/26 by Class N7 0-6-2 tanks (see earlier) but as late as 1957, J69 0-6-0Ts, which had 180lbs boiler pressure, were still being used between North Woolwich and Palace Gates, on passenger duties, and East Anglians who were already suffering from steam starvation, could still find some solace here. Later, when their condition had deteriorated, they found final, temporary relief on the Clapham Junction – Kensington trains, where it was still possible to be the only passenger on a rush hour steam train.

Britannia Pacific *Hereward the Wake* on an up Clacton express approaching Kelvedon, in 1960, while Class J15 0-6-0 No.65478 waits on the branch with the Tiptree Jam train. A housing estate has now been built over the track of the light railway on this site. Shortly after relaying the branch to the factory, traffic started to go by road; this change, it can be readily appreciated, had a very deleterious effect on the future of the branch line.

A Cambridge – Clacton via Sudbury excursion train near Bures hauled by Class B12/3 4-6-0 No.61546 – note the fireman's best Sunday cap. This branch joined the main line at Marks Tey. The last slip coaches on the former GER main line were for Sudbury, being slipped at Marks Tey until the outbreak of War in 1939.

LMS Tilbury 4-4-2 tank No.41949 entering Colchester on a Clacton train. Stratford at this time was having a very difficult job keeping the steam services going while electrification and dieselisation were taking place. Some of the displaced Tilbury tanks had found their way to Southend on the Shenfield line, but proved most unpopular. A few were fitted unofficially with GE Stratford-type injectors and three of these found their way to Colchester where they worked to Clacton and Ipswich. The driver of the train shown in this photo was a very short man who used to carry a block of wood about with him on which he would stand, to get a better lookout. Colchester shed is on the left; this must have been one of the most difficult in the system to work, particularly in the war-time blackouts.

Robin Hood leaving Colchester for Clacton in the late 1950s, just before the station was rebuilt. The Britannias were still maintained at Norwich under the supervision of Mr. Bill Harvey but those sent to Clacton could go wandering around the system for several days before returning home. What a pity they were never fitted with Giesl ejectors as Mr. Harvey wanted.

A photograph taken in March 1959 shows the official Ministry of Transport Inspection train leaving Thorpe-le-Soken for Frinton. Electric working was due to start four days later. The train was being propelled by BR 2-6-0 No.46469. There was apparently a strict caste system in force; the brass hats stood in their bowlers, with furled umbrellas on an upper platform. The lesser mortals stood below, bareheaded and *sans* umbrellas. Luckily it was fine. The leading coach is the Officers Inspection Saloon, built in 1909 as No.48 and the Clacton electrification was its last job. It was a very fine vehicle, still maintained in its original varnished teak complete with GER Crest. It was unfortunately broken up within a week of being withdrawn in 1961.

Class J15 0-6-0 No.65452 with a Darlington chimney, working a Colchester-Harwich train near Manningtree. The Stratford locomotive chimney store had been bombed during the war and Darlington had come to the rescue.

A Harwich train waiting in the bay platform at Manningtree with an ex-GN Class C12, at the head of a train of ex-GE six-wheeled coaches. In 1935, the year of the photo, 4016 was the only C12 on the GE section; shedded at Parkeston after short stays at several sheds in the Norwich area it did good work on the Harwich branch. The coach attached to 4016, No.61009, a six-wheeled compartment third, was built in 1897 as GE 729, and lasted until 1942. Up to the beginning of the war, GE six-wheelers were still attached to express trains in cases of overcrowding and I once rode in one at over 80 mph!

J15 0-6-0 No.65458 at Mistley, on the reversing spur.

J15 0-6-0 on the Harwich branch, coming up from Mistley Quay while a K3 Mogul from Parkeston waits at the signal. Before 1891 the Quay was reached by a junction from the up line just beyond the bridge shown in the background. This circled round the main line but the growth of traffic was such that a new line was cut out on the down side in order to reach the Quay by means of a headshunt. Mistley Quay has shared in the growth of East Coast ports but, regrettably, there was not enough traffic to warrant the use of a permanent BR shunter and the traffic has now drifted away to the roads, in spite of a railway-orientated management. When trains were reversed into the up sidings, the locomotive could not always hold a heavy train, which would begin to slip downhill and become derailed by the catch points, shown in the foreground of this photo. The wagon immediately in front of the J15 is an LNER steel coal wagon of the company's last design. The GER had built steel locomotive coal wagons similar to this but on Grouping the LNER had reverted to wooden ones. It took over ten years to reverse the trend again.

J39 0-6-0, working 'wrong line' on a ballast train in 1938, near Brantham. The photo was taken to show the site of the track used in the construction of the line, seen to the right. The line from Manningtree to Harwich can be seen in the far background, together with the incline down which traffic for Mistley Quay had to be worked.

A wet morning in the mid-1970s and the West Quay at Ipswich had just been opened as a freight liner depot. A class 03 diesel shunter had just arrived at Griffin Wharf with a train of grain wagons and it was taken off to give a helping push to another 03, which could not manage to move its train of loaded freightliners owing to the gradient and wet rail. When both locomotives tried to start there was a most spectacular bout of slipping and the train started to roll backward down the hill, although both the locomotives were in full forward gear. The banking engine slid back past a notice board which said 'No locomotives to pass this point' for about fifty yards. At the second attempt they just made the ascent. Many sidings on the Great Eastern had always been shunted by horses and there was a convalescent home for them at Bentley near Ipswich, where Lord Claud Hamilton owned a farm.

An Officer's special conveying Sir Richard Marsh, at the time Chairman of British Railways, on an inspection tour. He had been to Felixstowe and his special train is shown reversing at Westerfield Junction on its way to Lowestoft. On the left is the old Westerfield station, built in 1877 by Colonel Tomline for the Felixstowe Dock Railway, even though in the 1862 census Felixstow (as it was spelt then) was only composed of 118 houses, serving as home to 673 people. For the opening day, the engine driver was dressed like the Colonel's cook, the guard like his butler and the fireman as his gardener. In 1900, by the signal in the background, the boiler of a J15 0-6-0, standing on the Ipswich side of the level crossing suddenly exploded, to come hurtling through the air above the down side platform. To the right of the picture is where the Mid-Suffolk Light Railway planned to have its terminus, with a steam bus to take passengers into Ipswich by road. The first sod was cut by the Duke of Cambridge and six hundred and one guests sat down to a magnificent lunch, accompanied by two military bands. The gist of the Duke of Cambridge's speech was: "We are all in much too much of a hurry today". A patient of mine was a steward at the lunch and he once gave me a vivid picture of the scene. The Duke then continued on his special train to Orwell where he spent the weekend.

The Westerfield up distant signal, with LNER E4 2-4-0 No.7462 passing. Ipswich was a railway centre of some importance, the locomotive department at one time employing over 500 men. The usual express workings were for Holden B12 4-6-0s, first built in 1911, to come down non-stop from Liverpool Street in 90 minutes with a heavy train of about 14 bogies, composed of both the Norwich and Yarmouth portions. It was always said that, of the passengers travelling beyond Ipswich, two thirds were for the East Suffolk line and one third for Norwich. At Ipswich the train would split into two parts, for Norwich and Yarmouth South Town and Lowestoft. The East Suffolk line was one of three Dr.Beeching failed to close. The others were Edinburgh-Newcastle and the old GWR route to Birmingham.

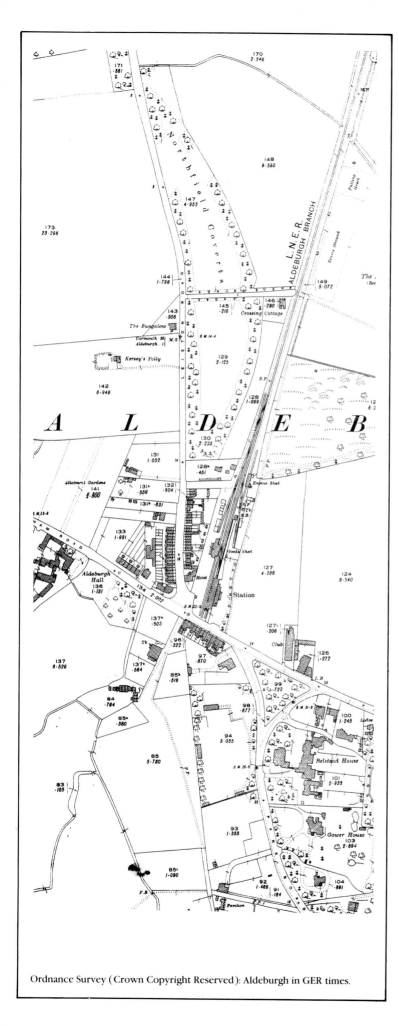

Ordnance Survey (Crown Copyright Reserved): Aldeburgh in GER times.

Above. J17 0-6-0 No.65511 on the Aldeburgh goods, returning to Ipswich. The Aldeburgh goods, like the Snape goods mentioned later, was a 'bonus' turn. This was a scheme copied from the North Eastern section to give the crew an incentive to get 'back home' as soon as possible. Otherwise it was very pleasant at the end of some desultory shunting to retire to the Station Hotel or the Great Eastern Arms for an hour or two. Even under the bonus scheme there was occasionally time to go blackberrying or to pick water-cress for the evening meal. The third van is an interesting Seddons Salt Wagon.

J15 No.65467 with an Aldeburgh branch train, coming to grips with the 1 in 53 out of Saxmundham.

Ipswich based B1 4-6-0 No.61052 on the down *Easterling* near Wickham Market Junction. *The Easterling* ran, in the summer months only, non-stop from Liverpool Street to Beccles. Here the rear three coaches for Lowestoft were detached, both parts going forward non-stop for the short final stretches. Once the regular maintenance of B1s broke down during the rebuilding of Ipswich shed, drivers preferred the best nominated Sandringham, No.61669, to a B1 for the train. A run-down Sandringham gave a very rough ride indeed and a B1 with its 6ft 2in wheels (those of the Sandringham were 6ft 7in) was preferred for starting heavy trains up the banks at Chelmsford, Colchester and Manningtree.

61660 *Hull City* still with its original 180lb boiler, leaving Wickham Market on an up express. The switchback nature of the track is clearly shown towards the back of the train. 61660 has suffered a bad case of 'priming' and may have been worked very hard as indicated by the burnt smokebox door and stains on the boiler. Such burns were unusual on these engines and might well be a result of not tightening the smokebox door properly – air would be sucked in, keeping the ash alight and glowing. The door would distort and gape, growing worse until the boiler makers clouted it back again.

Three cylinder Sandringham B17/3 4-6-0 No.61656 *Leeds United* passing Wickham Market Junction on a down Yarmouth express. The Sandringhams had been specially built in 1928 for the lightly laid track, with its weak GER bridges, replacing the smaller Holden B12s. The Sandringhams were very powerful machines but in order to keep weight down they were too lightly built for the power generated; they were not one of Sir Nigel Gresley's most successful designs.

Wickham Market was the station for the Framlingham branch, the actual junction being a mile down the line. This is the Framlingham branch train leaving the main line at Wickham Market Junction in 1946, behind an LNER F3 2-4-2T, No.7140. The coaches had originally been built for the *Norfolk Coast Express* in 1906. The junction was controlled by a lonely signal box, approached up a narrow lane. One Saturday night during the War a message was received that an urgent military special would be working to Framlingham early on the Sunday morning. There was only one staff for the branch, a heavy brass Annett key weighing seven and a half pounds which had already gone down to Framlingham on the last night train. The station master, therefore, had to go to the pub where the foreman was celebrating his birthday, and ask him to volunteer to cycle the seven miles or so down to the junction with the staff, without which no train could get on to the branch. Without a moment's hesitation he agreed and was therefore immediately plied with several more rounds of birthday drinks. He duly set off in the blackout but had to stop when he got to Parham where he propped his bicycle up against the river bridge! Here the staff fell into the fast flowing icy water. Again without a moment's hesitation he plunged into the torrent, where a few minutes later he was joined by a passing drunken reveller. As luck would have it, they were discovered by a very fussy Home Guard adjutant from a neighbouring unit, full of his own importance, who on hearing the babbling in mid-stream, in broad Suffolk dialect about a military special, thought he had discovered a couple of spies. He immediately arrested them and they were removed to GHQ under escort. Here sanity slowly returned and all were sent back somewhat crestfallen. They were accompanied by a detachment of troops in six armoured cars to assist in the location of the missing staff in the river. This was ultimately accomplished and an imposing convoy set off for the junction signal box. Here the unfortunate signalman was trying to explain to a disbelieving Inspector at Ipswich that the staff was apparently lost. Looking up to see six shadowy armoured cars coming down the lane in the blackout he jumped to the conclusion that the Germans had invaded at last, so he thought the only thing he could do was to go to the signal box steps with his hands above his head to surrender. This story has its origins in truth, but having been away at the time I cannot vouch for the strict accuracy of all the details....

F3 2-4-2T No.67127 leaving Wickham Market Junction with the Framlingham branch train. June 1949.

Above. J15 No.65478 on the Framlingham branch, with a weed killing train.

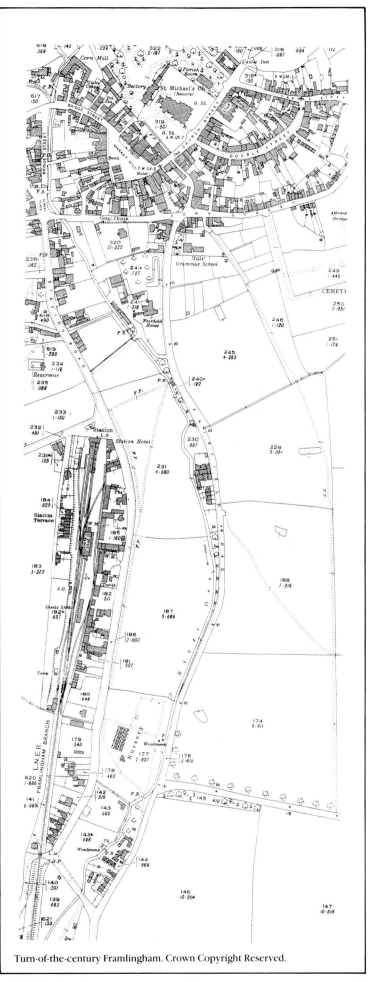

Turn-of-the-century Framlingham. Crown Copyright Reserved.

65459 on the Framlingham College special train, at the beginning of term, May 1955. Near Framlingham.

Mr. Gerald Leedham, a Framlingham citizen, had once been General Manager of the Cheshire Lines Committee, and he persuaded British Railways, after the closure of the branch to passenger traffic in 1952, to run a special train at the beginning and end of term for Framlingham College (petrol was still rationed). This is one such train, being hauled by Class B12/3 No. 61564, a rebuild of one of Holden's small B12 4-6-0s. With proper maintenance these were very fine locomotives with a very good route availability, some drivers preferring them to a larger Sandringham. All went well until April 1958, when the J15 rostered for the end of term special required to blow up at Framlingham for an unconscionable time, thereby missing all the connections. Attack is always the best form of defence and, when the bursar arrived at his office next morning, about to lodge a complaint with BR, an official was already there to tell him the College could never have another special, as they no longer had any spare coaches.

F6 2-4-2 tank No.67239 working an up mixed train off the Framlingham branch. The previous day the branch engine had become a total failure and 67239 had been hurriedly sent out from Ipswich to the rescue. It was very rare for the branch engine to be working chimney first in the up direction, as hand coaling by night normally required that it always worked out of Framlingham bunker first. Coaling and cleaning by night was a lonely job – at least one unfortunate worker suffered a nervous breakdown. The 1947 suburban electrification had freed the F6 2-4-2Ts from the suburban services for a more leisurely life in the country, replacing the F3s previously used.

D16/3 4-4-0 No.62552 in July 1951. The train is a Sunday Framlingham – Liverpool Street excursion, stopping to pick up passengers at Hacheston Halt. A pair of household steps from Framlingham station house (see also Frontispiece) was carried in the guards van, held in position by the obliging guard.

J15 No.65469 propelling the Eastern Region General Managers special train over the Framlingham branch, near Parham in April 1961. This was the last time a steam locomotive worked over the branch.

Doctor's privilege. The author at Laxfield, guest of driver Joe Skinner. The period is near the end of the Light Railway's existence and the train one of the GE suburban sets. Photograph by Harold James.

Super Claud, 4-4-0 No.62590 on the Framlingham branch train near Framlingham. It was a memorable occasion. I was driving past Wickham Market station one evening when I saw the London express running in, but there was no sign of life whatsoever from the branch train. I parked my car and went to investigate, finding all the crew asleep in a compartment. The previous day had been their rest day and they were all tired. I woke them up and investigation showed a boiler pressure of only 60 lb – insufficient to work the vacuum brake. Fortunately the station and siding were on a 1 in 100 down gradient, so after releasing the brake by hand, using the cord, the train rolled into the station by gravity and stopped on the hand brake. It then rolled the mile down to the junction where the fireman picked up the staff, and got out of sight of the main line before stopping for a blow up. The guard went down the train apologising for the delay which he said was due to the poor coal British Railways had supplied them with. But, he said, they would do all they could to make up any delay once they started – and they certainly did! I have never ceased to thank The Almighty for guiding me to a practice which had such a branch line, not to mention the fact that at the other end of my practice was the terminus of the Mid Suffolk Light Railway. 62590's whistle has survived to be the centrepiece of many an Ipswich dinner table!

Hacheston Halt with another excursion train hauled by Claud No.62526. This was Ipswich's 'other Claud', the first one being No.62590, the Belpaire one mentioned above. Normally this engine worked locals to Cambridge, due to its temperamental steaming. When these excursions returned in the dark, trying to locate the Halts like Hacheston, lit by a single oil lamp, was very difficult.

The Snape goods leaving Snape, behind No.65433. The J15 was the only class of locomotive allowed to cross the typical trestle bridge. At the end of the War, when Ipswich could not always supply one of these 0-6-0s, the Framlingham branch F3 2-4-2T was allowed down in an emergency. Jock was in charge at Snape, which had no railway telephone line – only a GPO one, so he never knew when a train was coming. I have often seen him swimming in the river when the train would rattle in over the bridge dropping cinders on to his head. He then would have to climb quickly out (a bonus train could never be delayed) sinking deeply into the mud, and cope with the shunting. In the sugar beet season, the Snape goods was always heavily loaded when it left Woodbridge. The Maltings can be seen on the right, now known to so many music lovers. The locomotives employed on the bonus trains required much more servicing than those on normal traffic...

Above. 65478 shunting at Snape in August 1952. Being a bonus job there was never the usual time to arrange a nicely posed photo.

Left. The Snape goods reversing down the branch on a wintry day behind J15 0-6-0 No.65478. Snape dealt in its heyday with more sugar beet than any other station on the GE section.

B1 4-6-0 No.61001 *Eland* at Snape Junction working a down stock train. She was only stationed at Ipswich for a short time and was not a 'regular'. Snape itself was reached by a one and a half mile branch which left the main line by a trailing junction from the up road, down a 1 in 53 gradient. The train is made up of LMS and GWR milk tankers and then an LNER four-wheeled pigeon van. This is followed by an LMS Stanier full brake, then a Gresley bogie pigeon van and finally an SR parcels and miscellaneous van.

J17 0-6-0 No.65578, as fitted with J20 chimney on the Snape 'bonus' goods, near Wickham Market, April 1951.

The Civil Engineers steam crane on its final duty at Saxmundham, on a Sunday morning in 1981. It should have been on its way home before daylight but water suddenly started pouring from an unexpected source. The County Council water representatives had to be called and it was daylight before the culprit was found to be a railway main, which used to feed the water column used by the Aldeburgh branch locomotive. On summer Saturdays, Ipswich had to provide a tender locomotive for the Aldeburgh branch so as to prevent the main line being blocked by engines taking water. One Saturday morning the locomotive supplied was a Class J20 0-6-0.

Class B12/3 4-6-0 No.61564 at Saxmundham Junction, with the fireman about to give up the staff. The train is a Sunday excursion from Aldeburgh. The last two coaches are the special articulated stock built in the 1930s for excursion traffic. They were not so comfortable as the standard main line stock. This was the only occasion I ever saw the Saxmundham branch distant signal pulled off.

This photograph shows the usual Aldeburgh branch train, hauled by F6 2-4-2 No.67220 and the normal train of Gresley vehicles; in the foreground is *Sirapite*, the Richard Garretts works shunter. This is Leiston, where Garretts had their works, with extensive sidings supplying a lot of traffic to the branch. During the railway strike of 1919 Garretts staff worked the service on the Aldeburgh branch. *Sirapite* was an Aveling & Porter locomotive, which is now preserved – it makes a fascinating comparison with the F6. The only time I ever saw an E4 2-4-0 on the branch (except for a garden-judging special) was a substitute for the customary 2-4-2T. The East Suffolk line from Yarmouth to Ipswich had originally been laid very cheaply, with a minimum of earthworks and many level crossings. Before anybody had heard of Dr. Beeching and his axe, British Railways had set about emasculating the line, withdrawing completely in November 1959 the service from Beccles to Yarmouth South Town. Later, Dr. Beeching proposed to close the whole line from Westerfield Junction to Lowestoft, thus leaving half the county without any rail connections nearer than 25 to 30 miles – the half which had always been the most populated. The Romans fortified Dunwich, and Boudicca was always a local East Suffolk heroine. Later the East Suffolk countryside had to be protected from the marauding Norsemen. Orford Castle was strongly protected with this end in view. The result was a great number of villages close together but no large town to attract Inter City services. In addition to the historical aspects of the county, there was also the geographical – the many waterways restricted the development of the road system, creating bottlenecks where the roads crossed them. Aldeburgh and Woodbridge were both thriving ports with fifty trawlers plying from each. Coal was brought down by sea and the Woodbridge vessels took corn over to Liverpool and came back with salt from Cheshire. The coast belt thus had a much higher state of civilisation than inland. It would seem that the Central Electricity Generating Board's decision to build a nuclear power station at Sizewell, on the former Aldeburgh branch, saved the line. Twenty years after singling of the permanent way was first proposed, by Gerald Fiennes, General Manager Eastern Region, it was ultimately carried out for much of the route from Ipswich to Saxmundham and relaid with track reclaimed from the closed GN and GE joint line from Spalding to Whitemoor. The line had now been modernised with radio signalling and automatic crossings.

Halesworth station in the 1950s. The up train is collecting loaded tanks from the milk depot in the background, hauled by rebuilt Claud No.62597. In the foreground is the Halesworth milk pilot, 2-4-0 No.62797; on loan to Lowestoft it ran to and from Halesworth light engine daily, except for working a passenger train from Beccles to Lowestoft on Saturday afternoons. I once worked out that it ran 36,000 miles light engine in the course of this duty. The signal box was manned by Mr. Peter Punchard, whose father, grandfather and great grandfather had all been signalmen at Halesworth before him. Few people can have done more for Halesworth than Peter. He finally bought the signal box from British Rail and it is now saved for posterity together with a working signal, in the grounds of Halesworth School. Behind the signal box was the terminus for the old 3ft gauge Southwold Railway. I can remember Peter's father telling me how sometimes in the past when the old Southwold Railway tank engine could not climb the final ascent to the terminus, because of wet autumnal leaves on the track, the two horses

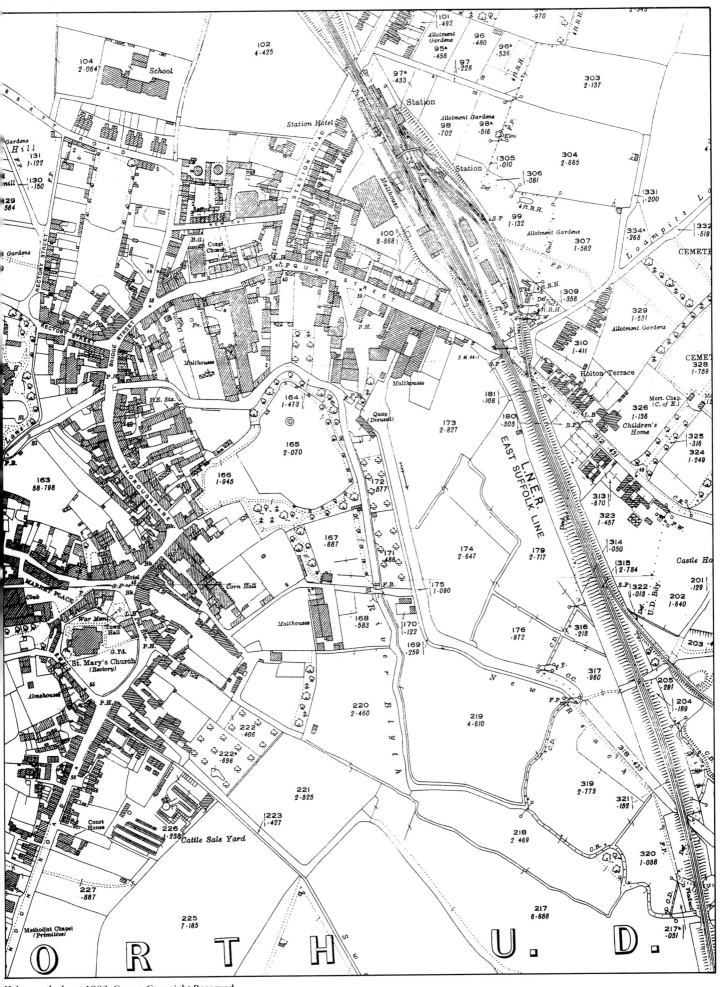

Halesworth about 1903. Crown Copyright Reserved.

Beccles was the junction where the Lowestoft coaches were detached, the main train usually running on to Yarmouth South Town. On a summer Saturday morning Beccles was incredibly busy. Britannia 4-6-2 No.70005 *John Milton* has just arrived at Beccles from Yarmouth South Town, picking up the Lowestoft coaches which had been brought in by L1 2-6-4T No.67701. The old GER had always tried to serve the public, the branch lines being regarded as feeders for the main line – not suckers as today. As well as the through Lowestoft coaches, there were the same facilities at Saxmundham from Aldeburgh, and at Westerfield Junction from Felixstowe.

B12/3 4-6-0 No.61514 leaving Beccles for Yarmouth South Town, passing the old engine shed. The coach next to the locomotive is an ex-GCR 12 wheeler, followed by a GER 54ft 3rd, a GE 50ft 3rd class Restaurant Car built for the Norfolk Coast Express, being used as a 3rd (as no dining facilities were advertised on the train), then 2 teak LNER coaches and, lastly, an LNER steel panelled coach.

The Lowestoft through coaches from Liverpool Street, leaving Beccles behind F6 2-4-2T No. 67232. These and their F5 counterparts did wonderful work out of Lowestoft, humble and elderly tanks given a new lease of life through care and special attention.

Sunday excursions had always been very popular in East Anglia and the Waveney Valley branch from Tivetshall to Beccles was no exception. The first post-War excursion was composed of two quint-art sets made redundant by recent suburban electrification. The acute discomfort of these coaches was resented and the next excursion was made up of eight heavy main line corridor bogies, weighing full about 300 tons. This was a disaster, being too much for the small J15 0-6-0 provided. After considerable delay a pilot was sent out to the rescue from Lowestoft. Even more delay was then caused by the Beccles swing bridge – jamming in the heat just after the excursion train had left Beccles. The train had then to reverse on the wrong line and go to Lowestoft. Here the engines ran round and went to Haddiscoe, reversing up the loop to Fleet Junction finally to arrive extremely hot and late at Yarmouth. All further excursions were then double headed as shown here, E4 No.62789 piloting 0-6-0 No.65471. The Waveney Valley branch bridge over the river at Beccles was weak and the locomotives allowed over it very restricted. Class F4 and F5 2-4-2 tanks were permitted, but not Class F6. The state of the swing bridges at Beccles and Haddiscoe on the main line was blamed by British Rail for causing the closure of the Beccles-Yarmouth section, but they had been built as recently as 1926.

No.61329 passing Haddiscoe High level on its way from Beccles to Yarmouth. In the immediate left foreground a loop ran down to Marsh Junction on the line to Lowestoft. A friend who used to travel daily to school, from Somerleyton to Yarmouth, told me that the train ran round the curve on to the swing bridge (which was then single track) and reversed into the high level platform. In the reverse direction the train ran into Haddiscoe High level and then reversed before going forward round the loop to Marsh Junction. In the background (left) is Fleet Junction, and through a gap in the houses can be seen the Haddiscoe low level platform. The typical position of a GER distant signal will be noted. This photograph was taken during a partial eclipse of the sun.

B1 4-6-0 No.61058, an Ipswich engine, approaching St. Olaves. The old Great Eastern signal looms uncertainly above, and the insulated fish containers extending down the siding recall one of the line's principal traffics.

Yarmouth South Town engine shed. The two lubricators will be noted on 61670 *City of London*. They had been fitted when she was streamlined and *East Anglian* was similarly fitted. In the foreground is a push-pull N7, No.69696. The shed master here was Mr. W.A.Hardy; with Richard Hardy at Ipswich and D.W.Harvey at Norwich, messages went everywhere!

Above. F6 2-4-2T No.67234 standing at the Fish Dock loading platform at Lowestoft, shunting a train of fish vans – note the express head code.

Left. Vacuum fitted J17 0-6-0 No.65588 passing Civil Engineers Departmental loco No.40 outside Lowestoft loco shed, in August 1959. The coaches are to form an up express, and would be attached to the Yarmouth train at Beccles.

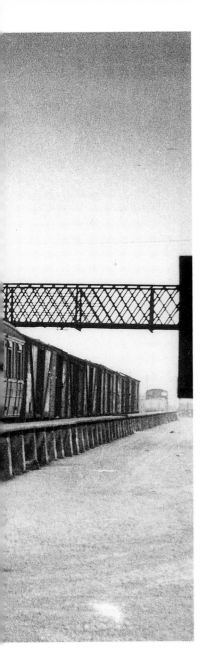

Sentinel shunter coming out of Commercial Road in Lowestoft, on its way to the docks. It is lettered 'Civil Engineers' Departmental Locomotive No. 38'. In recent years it was one of the most dramatic sights in East Anglia to see a £250,000 track machine running along Commercial Road to the track machine repair depot, preceded by a man waving a red flag. Unfortunately this has now been closed, along with the coal concentration yard, leaving only an occasional grain or oil truck to use the railway facilities of this thriving East Coast port.

The 'Pets Food Special' crossing the main road (once the main A12 road to the East Coast) outside Lowestoft station, behind 03 diesel shunter No.2018. Until recently the railway was a common carrier – that is, it had to accept whatever freight was offered. So, while every fish that left Lowestoft went by road, the railway had to accept the two trucks daily of fish offal which the road hauliers refused to handle owing to the offensive smell. These had to be marshalled well away from the guards van as they travelled up the joint line to the factory at Hull overnight.

Rebuilt Claud No.62570 entering Gorleston Links Halt, deputising for a failed push and pull locomotive. The Links Halt was an open station, normal practice today but very rare in the fifties.

The GER had a virtual monopoly of the railway system in East Anglia. Its only rival was on the North Norfolk coastal belt where the Midland and Great Northern Joint, a Derby orientated line, had managed to protrude tentacles as far south as Yarmouth and Lowestoft. The M & GN was a godsend to railway minded travellers who found that they could travel from Euston to Yarmouth via Rugby and Peterborough, for the same fare as that from Liverpool Street. But it was always an anathema to the old GER management, who managed to shut nearly the whole line in 1959, without waiting for Dr. Beeching. One of the results of this closure was that the still very considerable freight traffic for Norwich City (M & GN) had to travel via Norwich Thorpe – Cromer Junction and Melton Constable – a journey of 61 miles to do 1 mile as the crow flies. To halve this distance a loop was constructed in 1960 at Themelthorpe, to join the Norwich – Melton Constable line of the M & GN with the County School – Wroxham line of the old GER, the track bed of the latter from Themelthorpe to Reepham having to be repurchased, as it had already been sold. This loop was very short-lived being closed after about 20 years. The plate shows a Class 37 Diesel No.6726 on the loop, returning to Ipswich and the Norwich line.

J17 No.65512 on a down Norwich freight train passing Haughley. It is fitted with a small tender which made it extremely handy for backward running when turning was impossible. On the left is the grain silo built after World War Two on the site of the former Mid Suffolk Railway terminus. In the middle distance behind the station is a rebuilt Midland Railway tender, which once belonged to Lynn and Fakenham Railway 4-4-0 No.25. Built by Beyer Peacock in 1883, it had arrived at Laxfield freshly painted 'LNER' on January 1st 1948, the first day of British Railways, to serve as a mobile water tank. If you scratched away the upper layers of paint, it was possible to expose the original M & GN yellow. Unfortunately it missed preservation by only 24 hours. From 1928 – 1968 the down Liverpool Street to Peterborough mail (with a GPO van for Norwich) and the up Peterborough – Liverpool Street mail both met the Norwich mail at Haughley, where a great deal of remarshalling took place between 12.30 a.m. and 1.00 a.m. before the up and down mails went on their way and the Norwich mail returned home. For passengers who had to travel, these night trains were always greatly appreciated – especially during the 1939-45 War. The passenger facilities were withdrawn because BR said there were no longer any suitable coaches for them.

B12 4-6-0 No.8522 on a down Norwich express near Barham in 1936. Those engines were remarkably successful though, being small and lightly built they had to be changed at Ipswich in order to keep the fireboxes clean. Fifty of this class were fitted with the French ACFI system of feed water heating, which disfigured their good looks.

The through afternoon Stowmarket – Laxfield train (for school children) in the charge of J15 No.65459, reversing on to the branch at Haughley in June 1950.

An up express near Haughley Junction, hauled by K1 2-6-0 No.62034. These were mixed traffic locomotives being used for freight services during the week and for passenger services at the weekend, particularly in summer. This was a cause of some considerable friction; Stratford would habitually 'fail' the Moguls on a Friday night, denying their return to March. To the latter's fury the engines would promptly appear on Saturday mornings, sailing confidently off to Yarmouth and Lowestoft... They were the tender counterpart of the L1 2-6-4 tanks. In the foreground is a pair of catch points so that if any unbraked vehicle broke away and started running down the hill, it would be derailed before causing any damage.

J15 0-6-0 No.65442 entering Haughley on a Bury St. Edmunds – Ipswich train. The tender is of interest in that it is believed to be a 3000 gallon example, built between 1878 and 1881 by the then CME at Stratford, Massey Bromley, for one of his 4-2-2 singles. These had very short lives of only about ten years. Massey Bromley was killed in the Penistone railway accident of 1884: as far as I can make out, the only man who had ever been a CME to meet such a fate, though Wilson Worsdell, the Darlington CME, once had a very near miss in a snow plough accident.

Taken from the top of the silo, this photo shows a down Norwich express passing Haughley signal box, hauled by a B1 4-6-0. The line to Bury St. Edmunds, Cambridge and Ely bears away to the left, clearly showing the points by which the up Peterborough mail used to reach the down side island platform. Twice during the War a heavy ammunition train got out of control coming down the bank. Quick work by the signalman diverted them into the down island platform road and apart from bombs lying littered about the road at the Ipswich end of the station no serious damage was done. The track of the Mid Suffolk Light Railway can be seen away to the right up the 1 in 43 gradient over one of only three bridges on the line. The yard is full of material required for the extensive relaying of the Norwich main line going on at the time. During the last War, to cope with the extra shunting involved in extending the goods yard at Haughley, the first half mile of the light railway was strengthened.

J39 0-6-0 No.64894 on the 1 in 43 gradient – the underbridge can be seen in the previous photo. The second wagon is of some interest, being an LNWR gunpowder van.

Geoffrey Chaucer on an up Norwich express passing J15 No.65447 at Haughley. The 0-6-0 is waiting for a run down to Stowmarket, to pick up children who used the light railway to go daily to and from school.

BR Gas Turbine locomotive No.18000 waiting for the road at Haughley in January 1965. It was on its way back to the continent via the Harwich train ferry and, being out of gauge, progress was slow. It had been on loan to the Western Region for several years.

Taken in 1952, just before closure, this photograph shows J15 0-6-0 No.65447, climbing the 1 in 43 gradient out of Haughley on the Mid Suffolk. The six-wheelers have gone, replaced by the suburban stock – acutely uncomfortable and with no lavatory accommodation. The GER six-wheelers were well provided for in this respect. Today's Sprinters only have one lavatory for 163 passengers.... Consternation was caused recently on a Parkeston Quay – Blackpool train when a passenger decided to wash her hair. When she was at last coaxed out of the lavatory compartment it was found she had used all the water!

Britannia 4-6-2 No.70036 *Boadicea* passing Norwich Trowse Lower Junction on the up *East Anglian* express, tackling the mile at 1 in 80 up to the Upper Junction. The first line to Norwich came in from Cambridge and Ely in 1845 and is seen on the right of the photo. The line from Ipswich to Norwich Victoria was built in 1849 and the connecting line from Norwich Trowse Upper to Trowse Lower Junction in 1851. This was always 'the branch' up to the Norwich electrification in 1987. What a wonderful photograph the *Norfolk Coast Express* would have made at this site. *Boadicea* had its usual load of 9 bogies weighing 320 tons.

The introduction of dmu sets at Norwich in 1956 caused many of the older locomotives to be laid up and this photo shows a Claud, three E4s and a J15 0-6-0 stored at Norwich Trowse. It had not been intended to use the E4s again but they were still required by Cambridge for the Colchester service, on account of their coaling by hand (at night) at Sudbury. During a bitter wintry spell in 1952, a patient of mine once had to coal a Claud Hamilton 4-4-0 with high sided tender by hand at Sudbury.

A great contrast with the 66-year old steam locomotive of the previous photo. It shows a long row of withdrawn dmus at Wymondham in 1973, awaiting breaking up by Kings of Norwich, after a working life of only about ten years. British Rail had closed the whole of the M & GN line in 1959 and the Yarmouth – Beccles line later the same year. Paradoxically many of the surviving dmus are still carrying on today after over 30 years; they have never had the credit they deserve for allowing passengers to see the track ahead.

Though the line connecting Trowse Upper to Trowse Lower Junction was built in 1851, some passenger trains from Ipswich still ran into Norwich Victoria until 1916, when it became a goods depot. Norwich had a thriving industry and freights used to work into East Anglia from Peterborough via the Ely avoiding curve. They would run through the closed station at Trowse and come to a stand at Trowse Yard signal box where a shunting locomotive would come on at the rear. The photo shows an 03 diesel propelling two trucks on the up main, past the signal box. The night freight train from Whitemoor has almost stopped on the down main, and another 03 shunter is waiting to back on. In steam days it was one of the most dramatic sounds in East Anglia to hear a heavy freight pounding up the bank to the Upper Junction, a J69 0-6-0 tank leading and the train locomotive, usually a K3 3 cylinder Mogul, working away at the rear.

Sometimes the freight trains for Norwich Victoria would have to wait in the down sidings at the Lower Junction. This photo shows J19 0-6-0 No.64643 which has come out from Norwich and is starting to bank its train up the hill, a J69 tank leading.

A heavy freight train at the top of the bank (see previous page) moving forward again to reach Norwich Victoria. It is being hauled by 4-6-2 *Oliver Cromwell*, now preserved at Bressingham (1989). Class J69 0-6-0T No.68555 is at the rear.

Whitemoor (March) was the last depot on the Eastern Region to be closed to steam, in the first week of December 1963. But on December 12th I suddenly heard that majestic sound – a steam engine approaching. It was an 8F 2-8-0 No.48752 on a pre-Christmas cattle train. It transpired that Whitemoor had had no suitable diesel locomotive to haul it, and of course the cattle could not wait. The first view is the whole train in the cattle sidings at Trowse station and the second shows the 8F shunting four of the wagons for onward movement to Reedham, for fattening the animals on the marshes. 48752 was one of a batch built by the Southern Railway at Brighton works for the LNER and transferred back to the LMS when the war was over.

The winter of 1962/3 was the coldest of the century, so far; one morning in January 1963, Whitemoor had a row of *eighteen* diesel locomotives unfit for use owing to frost. A week or two later, three Norwich surgeons were returning home by car in the early hours after a medical dinner, when they thought they heard the whistle of a steam locomotive. They all looked at one another but nobody would admit to hearing it. A little further on the level crossing gates were closed and, owing to the row of cars stopped ahead of them, they could see nothing, except that the eye surgeon thought he saw a wisp of steam. They were all very relieved the next morning to hear that three Class B1 4-6-0s had arrived at Norwich to act as mobile heaters – one at Norwich, one at Yarmouth Vauxhall and one at Lowestoft. Later another arrived at Ipswich. They moved round in rotation so that they got a boiler washout every fourth weekend. This photo shows one of these locomotives shunting a truck at Norwich loco depot, lettered 'Departmental Locomotive No. 19'. As their boilers were not insured for normal use, it will be noticed that the screw coupling has been removed.

This photo shows N7 0-6-2T No.69707, which had escaped from the London suburban services where most of the class spent their lives. 69707 was one of about six which did a great deal of varied work from Norwich shed. It is probable that this working was the hardest they were ever called on to perform – a 12 coach train from Newcastle weighing, loaded, about 450 tons. A short wheelbase locomotive was required with such a long train so as not to block the points at Yarmouth Vauxhall. It was routed via Berney Arms.

K3 2-6-0s. No.61827 is coming in with a local from Peterborough, No.61953 waits for signals, having come down from Norwich Victoria and another waits to bank its freight train up the hill.

In the early 1950s there was still petrol rationing and rail traffic to the Norfolk Coast resorts was heavy. Norwich had to supply locomotives for the Midland and Great Northern as well as those for its own section. So, rebuilt Claud Hamilton 4-4-0 No.62611, one of a batch of ten built as late as 1923, had to be pressed into service even though its running plate had received quite a hard knock. It is shown approaching Whitlingham Junction from Yarmouth Vauxhall, via Acle.

A dramatic moment at Whitlingham Junction when A5 4-6-2T No.69815, an ex-Great Central Railway locomotive, takes the curve on to the mile long 1 in 80 up gradient on the Cromer line. Cecil J. Allen in his book 'The Great Eastern Railway' writes of the down Norfolk Coast Express that 'liberties in speed used to be taken over the divergence on to the Cromer branch at Whitlingham Junction.' GC locomotives were allowed east of Whitemoor but not south. Norwich had an allocation of three A5 tanks but these had been specially cut down to suit the GE loading gauge. No.69815 was the only one of its class that I ever saw on the Cromer branch that had not been cut down. It was hauling a load of 11 bogies.

The Cambridge spare Royal engine B2 rebuilt 2-cylinder 4-6-0 No.61617 *Ford Castle,* diverging on to the Berney Arms line near Reedham swing bridge. It is hauling a Saturday Cambridge – Yarmouth train. Its regular driver, Bill Last, is on the footplate. He much preferred the original, unrebuilt, *Sandringham.*

Yarmouth Vauxhall – Norwich via Berney Arms train entering Reedham Junction behind rebuilt Claud No.62586. To save train movements in Norwich, many Yarmouth and Lowestoft trains ran combined to and from Reedham Junction. In this photo two Clauds are waiting in the siding, to be attached to trains that split here. At the time of writing there is still a dmu which comes in from Yarmouth to Reedham Junction to make connection with Lowestoft trains.

The original line from Norwich to Yarmouth Vauxhall was via Reedham and Berney Arms, opened in 1844, a special train conveying a brass band, in the coach next to the engine, whose favourite tune was *See the Conquering Hero Comes*. The line from Reedham to Lowestoft followed in 1847 and later, in the 1880s, the line from Yarmouth to Brundall via Acle. This photo shows a train from Yarmouth Vauxhall to the Midlands coming off the Acle line at Brundall, hauled by K3 2-6-0 No.61877. From its headcode it will be taking the Wensum curve, thus avoiding Norwich.

K3 No.61834 on the Bury St. Edmunds line with a Parkeston – Whitemoor freight composed mostly of continental ferry wagons. These were always a great contrast compared with the traditional British short-wheel-based ones. The second vehicle is an 'Interfrigo' van.

A Suffolk Hunt special at Mellis. These workings were very popular with Hunts, in the heyday of the railway before the coming of cars, but not so popular with Railway Management. The latter could not control the destination of the special which was in the hands of the fox – the special had to go where he wanted and the signalmen had to do the best they could. The occasion of the resurrection of this past practice, in 1957, was the petrol rationing caused by war with Egypt, over the Suez Canal. The train is composed of two Gresley brake thirds and nine LMS horse boxes, and an LMS Special Cattle van for the hounds. The GER used to have a specially converted coach for carrying fox hounds. On this occasion Claud 4-4-0 No.62615 had just arrived at the Eye branch platform at Mellis from Bury St. Edmunds after reversal at Stowmarket. British Railways had made a great effort in order for the day to be successful and had provided horse boxes from Newmarket together with the senior horseman. The locomotive was in perfect condition having been used the previous day on the Royal train from Wolferton to Kings Lynn. The Southend electrification had taken place in December 1956 and the B12/3 4-6-0s previously used there had been sent to Cambridge to replace the Clauds, owing to their better weight distribution. It was said that the previous day's working on the Royal Train was probably the last for a Claud. There were a few more Royal steam workings but it is thought these were hauled by N7 tanks.

The next station after Wymondham heading towards Ely is Spooner Row, where Britannia No.70003 *John Bunyan* is pulling away from a signal check. Spooner Row is one of a series of small stations on the Ely – Norwich line which thankfully are still with us. Spooner Row always had been extremely small, only ever having one siding and no cross-over, even in GE days.

Wymondham in 1936, with D13 4-4-0 No.8030 on a Norwich to Wells train, standing next to J15 No.7562. The latter had come in from Forncett and then reversed into the down platform to get out of the way of the Wells train. The Forncett – Wymondham line, of which photos seem very rare, was opened in 1881. With the small village of Ashwellthorpe the only station on the branch, it is difficult to see why it was built. It was closed to passenger traffic on the outbreak of War in 1939 and to freight in 1951. In the 1960s Kings of Norwich were using the branch to store and gut by fire large numbers of redundant rolling stock. They had gutted some coaches in the Norwich sidings and had nearly set the city on fire.

No.62570 on a Wells – Norwich train, entering Dereham in August 1953.

The afternoon Lowestoft – Whitemoor stock train leaving Dereham for King's Lynn, hauled by 4-4-0 No.62524. The engine has reversed by running round the loop seen to the right of the photo. The Clauds were Route Availability 5 but they had special permission to work the Route Availability 4 section from Dereham to King's Lynn. Dereham was a thriving country railway centre, controlled by four signal boxes.

No.62524 again, this time leaving North Elmham on the daily milk train; the dairy is on the left and the buildings to the right form a granary. Rail traffic to it ceased in January 1989. On Sunday afternoon, this milk train used to carry passengers from Dereham to Norwich.

J17 0-6-0 No.65528, with small tender, passing Thetford West Junction where the line for Bury St. Edmunds branched off. No.65528 was the Bury branch freight engine and was returning from Roudham Junction where it had gone with a truck to connect with the Swaffham branch. Roudham Junction was an interchange platform in Great Eastern days where the last train from Swaffham connected with the Norwich train from Ely – there was no time for it to do this at Thetford.

Swaffham was a junction station on the line from Dereham to King's Lynn where the line to Thetford branches off. This is the Thetford branch train hauled by C12 4-4-2T No.67367 (a Doncaster built locomotive) piloting E4 2-4-0 No.62789 near Roudham Junction, where the line ran alongside Peddars Way. The piloting was caused by the unbalanced working of the school train. Watton was the most important intermediate station on this branch, serving both an Army and an RAF camp in the 1939-45 War.

F6 2-4-2T No.67236 on a Bury – Thetford train entering Thetford Bridge (shortly before closure) in May 1953. Like all East Anglian branches, this one carried a very heavy traffic in the 1939-45 War.

F6 2-4-2T No.67238, leaving the sidings at Thetford with the mid-morning Bury train, in May 1951.

65472 (pilot) and 67367, leaving Thetford with the mid-morning Swaffham branch train, in November 1953.

Sandringham No.61642 *Kilverstone Hall* leaving King's Lynn for Cambridge and Liverpool Street. King's Lynn and Hunstanton both had short turntables and the 'Footballer' Sandringhams could not be turned there, owing to their large tenders. In front of the signal box is a GE Travelling Gas Tank Wagon for gas-lit carriage stock, latterly used for carriage cooking equipment.

King George V died at Sandringham in 1936 and his body was conveyed by train from Wolferton to London. From King's Lynn, after reversal, it was hauled by No.2847 *Helmingham Hall* which had exchanged tenders with 2858 when the latter was renamed *Essex Regiment*. This is the Royal Train in 1931, near Cambridge on its way from Wolferton to King's Cross on a very blustery day. It is hauled by Super Claud No.8783 which, together with sister engine 8787, was kept at Cambridge in perfect condition for such duties. Both engines were later fitted with copper capped chimneys and, like the other Super Clauds, had the top feed apparatus removed. When King Edward VII was Prince of Wales he had a lady friend who built him a station, Easton Lodge, on the Bishop's Stortford – Witham branch where he used to visit her. He would travel in his special saloon coach. A patient told me that his grandfather's duty used to be to draw all the blinds in the saloon before they reached Bishop's Stortford.

Wissington in the factory complex, shunting two mineral wagons; quite a contrast to the open fields overleaf.

Hudswell Clarke meets GE.

On the way south from King's Lynn the line passed Denver Junction, just south of Downham Market. Here a branch forked towards Stoke Ferry, from which a privately built line ran eastwards from Abbey to Wissington and beyond, to serve the outlying Fenland farms. This line came into the ownership of the British Sugar Corporation to serve its sugar beet factory at Wissington. This is the Wissington Railway 0-6-0 tank *Wissington,* now preserved at Sheringham, running westwards over an apparently endless fen at Poppylot Farm; even today the roads in this fen area are liable to sudden subsidence.

An entirely spontaneous photo. I had seen the train coming from Abbey, where it had connected with the King's Lynn freight, when I suddenly heard a steam locomotive coming in the opposite direction on the single track. This was *Wissington* hurrying down to Abbey with a truck which it was hoped the freight train could take away back to Lynn before its departure. As *Wissington* came round a bend still steaming hard, the driver leaned right out of his cab to get a good view of the impending confrontation. Fortunately oil gave way to steam and a collision was averted. The diesel retreated into the nearest siding. I imagine this photo to be unique.

Class 40 No.D357 on a freight train at Ely North Junction with the signal off for the line to March and Peterborough. The line to King's Lynn went straight ahead and that to Norwich branched away to the left of the photo. Curving sharply round to the right is the line which gives through running from King's Lynn and Norwich to March and Peterborough. Ely Cathedral stands in the background. The only passenger trains to use the North Curve today are a few Saturday summer trains from the Midlands to Yarmouth. The Sprinters which have taken over all the cross-country services now run in and out of Ely.

Waterbeach, with B12 No.8536 fitted with the ACFI feed water heater mentioned earlier. The coach immediately behind the tender is of interest. It is NER designed on LNER bogies, built at York specially for the GE section. Travelling southwards from Ely a line immediately branched off to Bury St. Edmunds and Newmarket. The *North Country Continental* from Parkeston Quay to York and Liverpool was the most important train to use this line. The Newmarket horse traffic was also a very good source of revenue.

The Mildenhall freight leaving Quy station for Cambridge. Latterly this train only ran three days a week, the line being closed completely in 1965.

A passenger waiting for a train at Worlington Golf Links in 1961, Mildenhall being a mile down the line on the left. The Mildenhall branch was closed to passengers in 1962. For its last few years it had been worked by a dmu and the guard had to be very gallant in helping passengers off and on the train. In steam days there was a pair of steps worked by air connected to the braking system like that on the Framlingham branch train at Hacheston Halt.

An up King's Cross buffet car train leaving Cambridge in 1932 with eight main line bogies, hauled by D15/2 No.8866. It was a wet September evening and this must have been one of the hardest duties an unrebuilt Claud was ever called upon to perform. With three stops it was allowed 72 minutes to London. No.8866 was one of Cambridge's best locomotives, both unrebuilt and as rebuilt with 8 inch piston valves in 1933. The piston valve rebuilds were the best of the Claud Hamiltons by a very long way.

This photo was taken at Fordham Junction and shows, unusually, a D16/3 Claud, No.62584, being run in on a freight train after a winter spent in store. The Mildenhall branch can be seen coming in from Cambridge on the right.

B12 No.8530 just south of Trumpington with a lovely selection of vans on a parcels train. Immediately behind the tender is an LNER 'general van' built for the GE section, then a Gresley four-wheeler and then a magnificent variety of GE ones.

Also taken just south of Trumpington (where the LNWR route ran into Cambridge) this photo shows one of the K2s No.4652, allocated to the GE section; most of these including No.4652 were fitted with Westinghouse brake gear. The engine is working a Temple Mills – Whitemoor banana train. This traffic originated from Victoria Docks in London and then was tripped through to Temple Mills by a steam heated J69, to encourage the still green bananas to ripen enroute to their destination in the North. These engines then returned to London hauling coal. There were on occasion up to four of these special banana trains a day, in the years before the war.

A Cambridge – Colchester train leaving Long Melford, the junction for Bury St. Edmunds. It is drawn by E4 2-4-0 No.62784, an interesting engine with a tender originally designed for oil fuel, and one fitted with a window cab for working over the Pennines from Darlington to Penrith for a short time in the late 1930s, where it replaced GN 4-4-0s. It has a short Darlington chimney. The Bury St. Edmunds branch train is waiting on the siding and its own locomotive, a Doncaster built C12 4-4-2T had just failed. The J17 0-6-0 on the Sudbury – Cambridge freight was sent for and found to be fitted only with the steam brake. It was therefore placed ahead of the C12, to be responsible for the haulage of the branch train, while the 4-4-2T worked the brakes.

No.67237 entering Cockfield on a Long Melford – Bury St Edmunds train, July 1952.

Two engines at Long Melford, B2 *Castle Hedingham* and N7 No.69620. N7s were unusual at Long Melford; No.69620 was the last but one engine built at Stratford.

The 'Hat' train. In the 1950s there lived at Lavenham a lady who made 'Ascot Hats' that were very large. Nobody would carry them because of the inconvenience but BR as a 'common carrier' could not refuse so a special train had to be laid on and this is it, approaching Lavenham; J20 No.64696 with the hats in, curiously, an LNER fruit van with an LMS brake at the rear! It was these delightfully odd trains Dr. Beeching soon put a stop to.

Clare station on the Haverhill to Long Melford line was unique in Great Britain, being built in the grounds of a castle. This photo is also quite rare as B17s did not often work freight trains. No.61622 *Alnwick Castle* on a local goods at Clare.

At Haverhill the old Colne Valley and Halstead Railway ran through to Chappel, so that the Colchester via Sudbury train left Haverhill first and the Colne Valley train arrived at Chappel before it. This photo shows Ivatt 2MT 2-6-0 No.46465 on a Sunday Cambridge – Clacton excursion near White Colne. The track had been treated (unsuccessfully) with weed killer.

Two J20 0-6-0s at Whitemoor, Nos.64699 and 64691. Their great size is shown by the third locomotive in the row – an LMS 4F 0-6-0 which looks small in comparison. March, with its adjacent locomotive shed and marshalling yards, was always full of interest. I once had the privilege of being shown round the yards by night by the best guide I have ever met. At the end of the visit we were shown into the mess hut for a cup of tea. At first we had a very frigid reception, it naturally being assumed that the only people wandering about the yard by night must be official snoopers. But, when it was realised that we were harmless, we could not have been shown more kindness. I remember there was an animated discussion in progress as to whether one invited one's ex-girlfriend to one's wedding.

For a few years in the 1960s, there was a booked passenger train on summer Sunday mornings from Stamford to Hunstanton which took the March avoiding loop shown in this photo. It is hauled by a Brush type 2 diesel. In the 1950s there were fourteen trains booked into Hunstanton on a summer Sunday morning, the branch being one of the few where one could even see an ex-LMS 'Crab' 2-6-0.

Wisbech was on the March – King's Lynn line and from it there was a lineside tramway, which terminated at Outwell. In this photo a train is running along the road in the charge of an 04 diesel, D2202. One pouring wet Sunday afternoon a special, conveying passengers standing in 20 open trucks, worked over this line to the astonishment of passing motorists. One of the latter stopped his car to find out who we were and was told 'they are dissidents, Sir, going to the Labour Camp to be liquidated.' To which the motorist replied 'Jolly good show'.

There was also a harbour branch at Wisbech, which ran through a public park. An unusual feature of this was the fixed distant signal on a telegraph pole, dating from the 1914/18 War. This photo shows an 04 shunter with a timber truck and brake passing this peculiar survival.

North from Whitemoor ran the GN and GE joint line, to the coal fields; over it there would be an endless succession of coal trains – loaded south, empty wagons north. Cambridge engine shed alone required three coal trains a day. Murrow was the second station north of March on this line and this photo shows a Class 37 diesel about to cross the M&GN line from Peterborough to King's Lynn on the level. To deal with the brick traffic from Eye a new loop was put in over the site of Murrow station. The line to Eye was closed in 1966. The loop was also used for Wisbech until 1964, trains having to reverse at Murrow. It was used by two society specials using dmus in the course of its short history.

A WD 2-8-0 with two brake vans of LNER and LMS origin on the crossing, running on the M&GN line. The recently laid cut off spur is in the foreground.

Ex-GC Atlantic No.5266 at Huntingdon North (GN) Station. Such locos on the Great Northern Line were rare, apart from some on Cambridge buffet trains and locals between Hitchin and Peterborough.

Ex-LNWR G2 0-8-0 on a through freight heading for Peterborough, at Whittlesea, the only station between March and Peterborough. This engine is an appropriate reminder that at Peterborough the Great Eastern had an 'end on' junction with the LNWR, which continued on the line of what today is the Nene Valley Steam Railway.

North was the other Peterborough station, on the Great Northern line, and this is the station that survives today. Here, before the last War, is V2 2-6-2 No.4797. In the background is another GC Atlantic and to the left, in the distance, a GN one.

Another V2 at Peterborough in the last days of steam. This engine varies from the previous one in several ways – most noticeably by its double chimney. I was talking to the Peterborough 'New England' shedmaster about the diesels when this train passed. I asked him his opinion of them. 'I'm not sure about diesels' was his reply 'but I could do with a lot more of these' he said, pointing to the V2.

A lucky photo – the next station north of Peterborough on the GN main line at Essendine. While I was there I learnt that the 'Flying Scotsman' was due. I was due to catch the 'local' hauled by the GN Atlantic, so I asked the guard if I had enough time to get a photo of the 'Scotsman'. He looked at his watch, scratched his head and said 'you've got two minutes'. I ran over the footbridge got my photo and to my great delight *Flying Scotsman* itself was on the front. I ran back over the footbridge and got my train with a few seconds to spare!

Finally, the pre-War LNER's most prestigious train the 'Silver Jubilee'. This was all streamlined, complete with beaver tail observation car at the rear. This photo shows No.2510 *Quicksilver* hauling the train non-stop to Darlington at Essendine station, which explains the smoke. The driver has just 'eased' the engine a little going through the station on the climb up Stoke bank. A very fine sight.